How to Make
Purple Poop!

Witten by: Michael Langenfeld
Illustrations: Miriam.L

To order additional copies of this book, contact:
Xlibris
844-714-8691
www.Xlibris.com
Orders@Xlibris.com

ISBN: Softcover   978-1-6641-4511-5
        Hardcover   978-1-6641-4512-2
        EBook   978-1-6641-4510-8

Print information available on the last page

Rev. date: 11/25/2020

To my daughter Anya:
May you stay silly forever!

Chapter 1
The Question

One morning, my daddy came into my room and whispered, "Hey, I just had purple poop!"

"WHAT?" I said. "OMG, you are so funny Daddy."

"No, it's true! I ate beetroot yesterday and my poop was purple!" my daddy confirmed.

Now, I've seen black poop, brown poop and even green poop, but I've never seen purple poop before. "Does beetroot really make purple poop?" I wondered aloud.

Chapter 2
The Hypothesis

My daddy smiled and said, "Would you like to try and make purple poop too?"

"Daddy, you are so weird! Does beetroot really make purple poop?" I asked and tried to imagine what purple poop would look like. I couldn't help but laugh.

"Come on! It will be fun and a healthy experiment all at the same time." my daddy said.

"What? Healthy purple poop!" I shrieked. This was getting weirder and weirder by the second.

"We can use the scientific method and test our hypothesis." my daddy pleaded.

"What? Test our hippopotamus?" I repeated.

"HYPOTHESIS," he laughed. "A hypothesis is a prediction that scientists make about what might happen in an experiment."

"So, Daddy, what is our hippopotamus?" I repeated again.

"Hy-po-the-sis!" my daddy laughed again with a huge grin on his face.

My Hypothesis: If I eat enough beetroot, then my poop will turn purple.

Chapter 3
Conducting the Experiment

"That was easy," I said. "What's next?"

"Now, for the fun part. We get to conduct the experiment," my daddy explained.

"Kodak, what?" I asked.

"Not Kodak, conduct or test our hypothesis," my daddy repeated.

"How do we do that?" I continued.

"Scientist conduct or do experiments to discover whether something works or not," my daddy explained further.

"So, what do we have to do?" I asked excitedly.

Conducting the Experiment
1. Eat 1 ½ cups of pickled beetroot or drink a large glass of beetroot juice in the morning on an empty stomach.
2. Drink lots of water during the day.
3. Wait 12 to 24 hours to poop.
4. Poop and record your observations.

"Yuck! Beetroot taste like dirt!" I exclaimed. "That was painful, Daddy!"

"Oh, it wasn't that bad. Did you know, that beetroot is very healthy for your body? Right now, your body is thanking you for all the wonderful nutrients you gave it," my daddy explained.

"Yeah, yeah. What's next?" I asked impatiently.

"Well, we wait for 12 to 24 hours until you are ready to poop. After you poop, you need to record your observation," my daddy explained.

"What do you mean, record?" I enquired.

"You have to write down what you see or observe. Scientist collect information about what happened. They write down what they see. This is important because it helps them gather information to answer their question. What is our question again?" my daddy asked.

"Does beetroot make purple poop?" I quickly replied.

"Oh, yeah!" my daddy confirmed.

Chapter 4

Recording your Observation

24 hours later...

"Daddy, I need to poop!" I exclaimed.

"Don't forget to bring your pen and paper to the bathroom and write down what you see!" my daddy shouted.

5 minutes later... "OMG, it worked Daddy. You weren't lying. I have purple poop!" I screamed.

Chapter 5
The Conclusion

"So, did you answer the question you wanted to test?" asked my daddy.

"Yes, I am what I eat. Purple poop!" I explained.

"Ha, ha. Well, in a way you are correct, but we need to be a bit sciencier when writing our conclusion or ending," my daddy explained.

"How do we do that, Daddy?" I quickly asked.

"In the conclusion, we use the results of our experiment and write down if we can confirm or reject our findings. So did we prove our hypothesis?" my daddy asked.

"WE CAN CONFIRM OUR HIPPOPOTAMUS!" I quickly yelled.

Printed in the United States
By Bookmasters